BRILLIANT POWERFUL RESILIENT
UNLEASHING WOMEN IN BUSINESS EXCELLENCE

Bible Principles & Promises

For Women Entrepreneurs

DR. TSCHANNA TAYLOR

Author of *Brilliant, Powerful, & Resilient: Unleashing Women's Business Excellence*

Bible Principles & Promises

For Women Entrepreneurs

DR. TSCHANNA TAYLOR

**Author of *Brilliant, Powerful, & Resilient:
Unleashing Women's Business Excellence***

Brilliant, Powerful & Resilient:

Bible Principles & Promises for Women Entrepreneurs

Copyright © 2024 Tschanna Taylor®

Scripture quotation taken from the Amplified ® Bible (AMP), Copyright © 2015 by the Lockman Foundation. Used by permission. www.lockman.org

Published by:

Emerald Tree Press™, an imprint of Tschanna Taylor Enterprises

Cover Design, Typesetting & Editor:

Redefined Publishing Agency

ISBN for print version: 979-8-9863601-3-3

DEDICATION

This book is dedicated to you—the brilliant, powerful, and resilient woman entrepreneur.

To the dreamers who see beyond the horizon, to the builders who lay foundations with determination and grace, and to the warriors who face the storms with courage unwavering. This is for the visionaries who dare to imagine a better world and then set out to create it, for the trailblazers who pave new paths where none existed, and for the nurturers who understand that true strength lies in compassion and community.

You, who balance the myriad demands of entrepreneurship with the call to serve, lead, and uplift others, embody the essence of brilliance, power, and resilience. Your journey is a testament to the strength that resides within a woman fueled by faith and guided by divine wisdom.

May this book be a beacon on your path, a source of encouragement during trials, and a reminder of the victories ahead. It is an honor to walk alongside you in this journey of entrepreneurship, where every challenge met with faith becomes an opportunity for growth and every success a platform for impact.

Here's to you, for embracing your calling with heart and perseverance, for transforming obstacles into stepping stones, and for leading with light and love. May your ventures flourish, your impact deepens, and your legacy inspire generations to come.

Be Bold

Be Confident

Be Courageous

Be Brilliant

Be Powerful

Be Resilient!

TABLE OF CONTENTS

Bible PRINCIPLES & PROMISES

FOR WOMEN ENTREPRENEURS

Introduction

Embracing The Nehemiah Blueprint and the 10 Essential Pillars in Business

I n the heart of every woman entrepreneur lies a vision—a call to not only create and innovate but to also infuse her work with meaning, purpose, and a touch of the divine. This vision, much like the task given to Nehemiah to rebuild the walls of Jerusalem, is not merely about constructing something new. It is about restoration, resilience, and responding to a call that transcends the ordinary demands of business. Nehemiah's story, rich in leadership, faith, and strategic execution, serves as a powerful blueprint for Kingdom-driven women entrepreneurs today. It underscores the importance of clarity of mission, unwavering motivation, and a mindset anchored in faith—principles that are foundational to achieving success in business and in life.

The journey of building a business aligned with Kingdom principles mirrors Nehemiah's work in several profound ways. It begins with a *Mission* —a clear understanding of what God has called you to build. Nehemiah was clear about his mission to rebuild the walls of Jerusalem, just as you must be clear about the purpose and direction of your business. *Motivation* then fuels this mission, driving you forward with passion and perseverance, akin to Nehemiah's zeal for the restoration of his city.

A *Mindset* grounded in faith and determination is essential, enabling you to face challenges with the confidence that comes from knowing God is on your side. Nehemiah faced opposition and discouragement, yet his faith remained unshaken—a lesson in maintaining a positive and resilient mindset amidst the trials of entrepreneurship. Your *Message*, the unique value and vision your business brings to the world, must be communicated clearly, just as Nehemiah rallied the people of Jerusalem with a compelling call to action.

Building your business also involves identifying your *Members* (your team and supporters), creating a *Movement* (the impact and change you wish to see), *Monetizing* your offerings in a way that sustains your mission, effectively *Marketing* to reach your audience, *Management* of resources and operations with wisdom, and making strategic *Moves* that propel you towards your goals. These pillars are the bedrock upon which you can build a business that not only prospers but also contributes to the greater good of your community and the Kingdom of God.

It is worth noting that these ten essential pillars of business are elaborated upon in the book anthology titled *Brilliant, Powerful, and Resilient: Unleashing Women's Business*

Excellence. This companion piece serves as a foundational resource, offering deeper insights and practical strategies to implement these pillars effectively in your entrepreneurial journey.

As Kingdom-driven women entrepreneurs, we are called to build not just for our success but for the glory of God and the betterment of others. The Nehemiah blueprint, combined with the ten essential pillars of business, provides a comprehensive framework for doing just that. It's about more than building walls or businesses; it's about building a legacy that reflects our deepest values and God's plan for our lives. This book aims to guide you through integrating these timeless principles with practical strategies, enabling you to achieve success on your terms and make a lasting impact in your sphere of influence. Let us embark on this journey together, embracing our divine calling with brilliance, power, and resilience.

Dr. Tschanna Taylor

PART ONE

Seven Brilliant, Powerful, & Resilient Bible Principles

Principles are foundational truths or laws that guide behavior and decision-making. In the context of Kingdom-driven entrepreneurship, these principles are rooted in biblical truths that not only influence the way business is conducted but also ensure that the business aligns with God's will and purpose. They serve as a compass for entrepreneurs, guiding them toward success that is measured not just in profit, but in impact, integrity, and influence for the Kingdom of God.

The seven Brilliant, Powerful, & Resilient Bible Principles serve as a compass, guiding you through the ever-changing landscape of entrepreneurship with wisdom that is both ancient and eternally relevant. They are not just strategies for business, but blueprints for life, each rooted in scripture and reflective of God's Kingdom. These principles encourage you to lead with vision, manage resources with stewardship, persevere through adversity, serve with humility, innovate with excellence, foster community, and give generously. As you delve into each one, you will discover how they intertwine, creating a tapestry of guidance that is designed to elevate not only your business but also your spiritual journey. This exploration is an invitation to transform your entrepreneurial endeavor into a living, breathing expression of your faith, one that resonates with the power of biblical truth and the light of God's purpose for your life.

Vision and Faith

Vision and faith are about seeing beyond the present circumstances to what can be achieved through God's power. It's the ability to dream big and believe that with God, all things are possible. This principle encourages entrepreneurs to set ambitious goals and trust in God's provision and guidance. Scripture supporting this principle includes Hebrews 11:1, "Now faith is the assurance of things hoped for, the conviction of things not seen," and Proverbs 29:18, "Where there is no vision, the people perish: but he that keepeth the law, happy is he." These passages highlight the importance of having a God-given vision and the faith to pursue it, even when it's not yet visible.

Stewardship

Stewardship refers to the responsible management of resources entrusted to one's care, viewing everything as a gift from God. This principle emphasizes accountability, sustainability, and generosity. Entrepreneurs are called to use their resources wisely, invest in their communities, and operate their businesses in a way that reflects God's principles of stewardship. Luke 12:48 states, "For everyone to whom much is given, from him much will be required," reminding entrepreneurs of the responsibility that comes with the blessings and resources God provides.

Perseverance

Perseverance is the commitment to continue pursuing God's vision for your business, even in the face of challenges and setbacks. It's about resilience and the determination to keep moving forward, trusting that God will provide the strength and resources needed to overcome obstacles. James 1:12 offers encouragement in this area: "Blessed is the man who remains steadfast under trial, for when he has stood the test he will receive the crown of life, which God has promised to those who love him.

Leadership

Leadership in the Kingdom context is about serving others and leading by example, reflecting Jesus' model of servant leadership. It involves humility, integrity, and the willingness to empower those around you. Philippians 2:3-4 advises, "Do nothing from selfish ambition or conceit, but in humility count others more significant than yourselves." This principle challenges entrepreneurs to lead with compassion, empathy, and a focus on developing the potential in others.

Innovation & Excellence

Innovation and excellence are about striving to do your best and seeking creative solutions that reflect God's creativity. This principle encourages entrepreneurs to pursue quality in all aspects of their business, setting a standard that honors God and serves others well. Colossians 3:23-24 reminds us, "Whatever you do, work heartily, as for the Lord and not for men, knowing that from the Lord you will receive the inheritance as your reward." This underscores the importance of excellence as a form of worship.

Community & Relationships

Building strong relationships and a supportive community is essential for sustainable success. This principle highlights the value of collaboration, mutual support, and integrity in dealings with others. Proverbs 27:17, "Iron sharpens iron, and one man sharpens another," speaks to the importance of community in personal and business growth.

Generosity

Generosity is the willingness to give freely and abundantly, reflecting God's generosity towards us. This principle encourages entrepreneurs to look beyond profit, to impact their communities and the world positively. Acts 20:35 highlights the blessings of giving, "It is more blessed to give than to receive." Entrepreneurs are called to be generous with their time, resources, and talents, using their businesses as a vehicle for blessing others.

These seven Kingdom principles serve as a guide for women entrepreneurs to build businesses that are not only successful in worldly terms but are also aligned with the values of the Kingdom of God, making a lasting impact on the world around them.

Notes

Notes

Notes

PART TWO

21 Brilliant, Powerful, & Resilient Bible Promises

A promise, in the biblical context, is a declaration or assurance that God gives to His people, guaranteeing His presence, support, provision, or action in their lives or circumstances. For believers, including women entrepreneurs, these promises serve as a foundation of hope and faith, offering guidance, comfort, and strength as they navigate the challenges and opportunities of their entrepreneurial journey. Each promise from God is a testament to His faithfulness, encouraging us to trust in Him as we pursue our God-given visions.

Here are 21 promises from the Bible, each associated with a key word that resonates with the journey of a woman entrepreneur. *The Brilliant, Powerful, & Resilient Bible*

Promises are meticulously crafted to resonate with every facet of your entrepreneurial journey, offering a word of hope, strength, or guidance precisely when you need it. By pairing each promise with a specific scripture, it not only provides spiritual nourishment but also practical wisdom that can be applied in daily business activities. Whether seeking strength in moments of weakness, wisdom in decision-making, or peace amidst chaos, these promises stand as reminders of God's unwavering support and infinite resources available to you.

To integrate these promises into your entrepreneurial life, start by reflecting on each word and its accompanying scripture, allowing the Holy Spirit to reveal its relevance to your current circumstances. Consider journaling your thoughts and prayers related to each promise, focusing on how it applies to the challenges and opportunities you face in your business. Make it a practice to declare these scriptures over your life and work, either at the start of your day or in moments of need. This intentional engagement with God's Word will not only deepen your faith but also empower you to navigate the complexities of entrepreneurship with a sense of divine backing and purpose. As you embody these promises, you'll find that they become more than just words—they transform into tangible manifestations of God's grace, guiding you towards a business that flourishes under His providence and reflects His glory.

1. Strength

Word: Strength

Scripture: Proverbs 31:25 *"Strength and dignity are her clothing, and her position is strong and secure; And she smiles at the future [knowing that she and her family are prepared]."*

Explanation: This scripture highlights the inner strength and dignity of a woman, equipping her to face the future with confidence and joy. For the entrepreneur, this strength is foundational, enabling her to lead with integrity and resilience.

2. Wisdom

Word: Wisdom

Scripture: James 1:5 *"If any of you lacks wisdom, you should ask God, who gives generously to all without finding fault, and it will be given to you."*

Explanation: Wisdom is crucial for decision-making and navigating the complexities of entrepreneurship. This promise assures that God provides wisdom generously to those who seek it, guiding every step of the entrepreneurial journey.

3. Guidance

Word: Guidance

Scripture: Proverbs 3:6 *" In all your ways submit to Him, and He will make your paths straight."*

Explanation: This scripture promises divine guidance for those who acknowledge God in their endeavors. For the entrepreneur, it means trusting in God's direction to lead their business towards growth and success.

4. Provision

Word: Provision

Scripture: Philippians 4:19 *"And my God will meet all your needs according to the riches of his glory in Christ Jesus."*

Explanation: Entrepreneurs often face financial uncertainties. This promise offers assurance of God's provision, meeting every need according to His riches and ensuring the business thrives.

5. Peace

Word: Peace

Scripture: John 14:27 *"Peace I leave with you; my peace I give you. I do not give to you as the world gives. Do not let your hearts be troubled and do not be afraid."*

Explanation: During entrepreneurial challenges, this promise offers a peace that transcends understanding, allowing the entrepreneur to navigate business pressures without fear or anxiety.

6. Courage

Word: Courage

Scripture: Joshua 1:9 " Have I not commanded you? Be strong and courageous. Do not be afraid; do not be discouraged, for the Lord your God will be with you wherever you go."

Explanation: This scripture encourages entrepreneurs to act boldly and with courage, reassured by God's constant presence and support in every situation, from pitching ideas to navigating setbacks.

7. Success

Word: Success

Scripture: Joshua 1:8 *"Keep this Book of the Law always on your lips; meditate on it day and night, so that you may be careful to do everything written in it. Then you will be prosperous and successful."*

Explanation: Success in business is linked to meditating on and adhering to God's Word. This promise aligns spiritual obedience with prosperity, offering a blueprint for success that is both spiritual and material.

8. Protection

Word: Protection

Scripture: Psalm 91:11 *"For he will command his angels concerning you to guard you in all your ways."*

Explanation: Entrepreneurs face risks and threats, both seen and unseen. This promise of angelic protection offers reassurance that God guards every aspect of their lives and businesses.

✖ + ✖ + ✖ + ✖

9. Hope

Word: Hope

Scripture: Jeremiah 29:11 *"For I know the plans I have for you," declares the Lord, "plans to prosper you and not to harm you, plans to give you hope and a future."*

Explanation: This well-loved promise offers entrepreneurs assurance that God has plans for their welfare, not for harm, fueling hope for a prosperous future and the success of their ventures.

10. Endurance

Word: Endurance

Scripture: Romans 5:3-4 *" Not only so, but we also glory in our sufferings, because we know that suffering produces perseverance; perseverance, character; and character, hope."*

Explanation: This scripture speaks to the transformative power of challenges, highlighting how they develop perseverance. For the entrepreneur, enduring hardships is part of the journey, shaping character and fostering a hopeful outlook for the future.

11. Joy

Word: Joy

Scripture: Psalm 16:11 " *You make known to me the path of life; in your presence there is fullness of joy; at your right hand are pleasures forevermore.* "

Explanation: This promise assures that in pursuing God's path for her business, an entrepreneur will find not just success but also joy. It reminds women entrepreneurs that true joy comes from aligning their endeavors with God's will, ensuring a fulfilling journey.

12. Favor

Word: Favor

Scripture: Proverbs 8:35 *"For those who find me find life and receive favor from the Lord."*

Explanation: Seeking wisdom and God's presence brings life and favor. For an entrepreneur, this divine favor can open doors, create opportunities, and establish partnerships that human effort alone cannot, ensuring her business is marked by God's blessing.

13. Rest

Word: Rest

Scripture: Matthew 11:28 *"Come to me, all you who are weary and burdened, and I will give you rest."*

Explanation: Entrepreneurship can be exhausting. This promise invites women to find rest in Jesus amidst their busyness, offering rejuvenation and peace that the world cannot provide, ensuring they continue their work with renewed strength and clarity.

14. Renewal

Word: Renewal

Scripture: Isaiah 40:31 *"But those who hope in the Lord will renew their strength. They will soar on wings like eagles; they will run and not grow weary; they will walk and not be faint."*

Explanation: This scripture promises renewal of strength for those who put their hope in the Lord. For the entrepreneur, it's a reminder that even in times of fatigue or discouragement, trusting in God renews vigor, enabling her to soar above challenges.

15. Freedom

Word: Freedom

Scripture: 2 Corinthians 3:17 *"Now the Lord is the Spirit, and where the Spirit of the Lord is, there is freedom."*

Explanation: This promise speaks to the freedom found in Christ—freedom from fear, doubt, and the constraints that can hinder business growth. For the entrepreneur, it affirms the liberty to innovate, create, and lead in the freedom granted by the Spirit.

✖ ✦ ✖ ✦ ✖ ✦ ✖

16. Creativity

Word: Creativity

Scripture: Exodus 35:31-32 " This promise speaks to the freedom found in Christ—freedom from fear, doubt, and the constraints that can hinder business growth. For the entrepreneur, it affirms the liberty to innovate, create, and lead in the freedom granted by the Spirit."

Explanation: This promise highlights the creative gifts bestowed by God. It encourages women entrepreneurs to embrace their God-given creativity, utilizing it to innovate and excel in their businesses.

17. Understanding

Word: Understanding

Scripture: Proverbs 3:13 *"Blessed are those who find wisdom, those who gain understanding."*

Explanation: This promise values the pursuit of understanding alongside wisdom. For entrepreneurs, gaining understanding is crucial in making informed decisions, understanding market needs, and leading their businesses with insight.

18. Blessing

Word: Blessing

Scripture: Deuteronomy 28:8 *"The Lord will send a blessing on your barns and on everything you put your hand to. The Lord your God will bless you in the land he is giving you."*

Explanation: This scripture assures that God's blessing encompasses all areas of life, including business endeavors. Entrepreneurs can trust that their efforts, aligned with God's principles, will be blessed and fruitful.

19. Confidence

Word: Confidence

Scripture: Hebrews 10:25 " So do not throw away your confidence; it will be richly rewarded. "

Explanation: This verse encourages entrepreneurs not to lose confidence in the face of adversity. It promises that steadfast faith and confidence in God's promises lead to reward, inspiring women to pursue their business goals with boldness and assurance.

20. Love

Word: Love

Scripture: Hebrews 10:25 "So do not throw away your confidence; it will be richly rewarded. "

Explanation Love is foundational in all aspects of life, including business. This passage reminds entrepreneurs that while faith and hope are vital, love should be the driving force behind their actions—serving customers, leading employees, and impacting communities with the love of Christ.

21. Integrity

Word: Integrity

Scripture: 1 Corinthians 13:13 *"And now these three remain: faith, hope, and love. But the greatest of these is love."*

Explanation: This scripture promises divine guidance for those who acknowledge God in their endeavors. For the entrepreneur, it means trusting in God's direction to lead their business towards growth and success.

Notes

Notes

Notes

PART THREE

Brilliant, Powerful, & Resilient Entrepreneurs' Prayer

Heavenly Father, Creator of all things and the ultimate source of innovation and wisdom, I come before You as Your daughter, embarking on this journey of entrepreneurship. You have blessed me with a vision—a vision to create, to serve, and to glorify Your name through my work. Grant me the brilliance to illuminate the marketplace with innovative ideas that reflect Your creativity. Infuse my endeavors with Your power, that through every challenge and triumph, Your strength is showcased, empowering me to lead with courage and integrity. Bestow upon me resilience, that in moments of trial and uncertainty, I may stand firm in faith, unwavering in my commitment to the path You have set before me.

Lord, guide my steps with Your wisdom, that each decision I make may be aligned with Your will and purpose. Help me to steward the resources You provide with responsibility and generosity, impacting not only my sphere of influence but also extending Your kingdom's reach. In moments of doubt, remind me of the promises You have spoken over my life—the promises of provision, strength, and success. Let my business be a testament to Your faithfulness, a place where Your love and grace are evident in every interaction. As I navigate the complexities of entrepreneurship, keep my heart and intentions pure, focused on serving Your people and creating value that honors You.

I pray for the community of brilliant, powerful, and resilient women entrepreneurs with whom I share this journey. May we uplift and support one another, sharing in successes and shouldering burdens together, united in our purpose to reflect Your light in the business world. Bless our efforts, multiply our impact, and let our collective legacy be one of faith, hope, and love, inspiring generations to come. With gratitude for Your unending grace and guidance, I commit my entrepreneurial journey into Your loving hands. Amen

PART FOUR

Brilliant, Powerful, & Resilient Decrees & Declaration

As a *Brilliant, Powerful, & Resilient Female Entrepreneur, everything you have or don't have reflects how you think. All your life you have been bombarded by images, comments, and in environments that have caused your thinking to shift. Sometimes you may see the negative and not the positive. The decrees and declarations below will help you to reset your mindset back to what the Bible tells us. Write them down in your favorite journal, post them all over the house, next to your computer, even in your car. The more places you see them, the better. Watch your life change when your belief in what God said He was going to do shifts. The more you use and believe them, the faster the shift!*

I decree I am a brilliant, powerful, and resilient female entrepreneur, capable of achieving greatness.

My dreams are worth pursuing, and I will fearlessly strive to turn them into reality.

I decree I embrace challenges as opportunities for growth and will conquer them with determination.

Success is within my reach, and I will grasp it with unwavering confidence.

I am a trailblazer, breaking barriers and paving the way for other women in business.

I trust in my abilities, and my intuition will guide me to make wise decisions.

Failure is not an end but a stepping stone to my ultimate triumph.

I radiate positivity and inspire those around me to do the same.

Every setback I encounter is an opportunity to learn and come back stronger.

I decree I believe in collaboration and support other female entrepreneurs on their journey.

My business reflects my passion and dedication to make a positive impact.

I decree I empower myself by empowering others, creating a ripple effect of success.

My resilience is unyielding, and I will rise above any adversity.

I decree I celebrate my achievements, no matter how big or small, and recognize my progress.

I decree I surround myself with like-minded individuals who uplift and motivate me.

Confidence is my superpower, and I wield it with grace and humility.

I decree I am not limited by anyone's expectations but my own, and I will surpass them.

I decree I attract abundance and opportunities to further my business and personal growth.

I decree I balance work and self-care, recognizing the importance of nurturing my well-being.

Fear will not dictate my actions; I will take bold leaps and embrace uncertainty.

I turn obstacles into innovative solutions that fuel my success.

My authenticity and unique perspectives are assets in the business world.

I cultivate a mindset of abundance, knowing that there is enough success for everyone.

Each day is a chance to make progress, and I embrace it with enthusiasm.

I welcome feedback and view it as a tool for improvement, not criticism.

My resilience shines through, even in the face of setbacks and I emerge stronger.

My achievements are a testament to my hard work, dedication, and brilliance.

I honor my values and let them guide me in making ethical business decisions.

I decree I am a role model for future generations of female entrepreneurs, paving the way for their success.

I decree I take time to appreciate and celebrate my journey, acknowledging the milestones I've reached.

I decree I am part of a powerful community of female entrepreneurs, united in strength and excellence.

I decree my products and services are in high demand and sell daily.

I decree customers buy my products and services because they recognize the value added to their lives.

I decree my products and services are worth full price.

I decree I build relationships and purchases follow.

I decree I am an excellent and integrous salesperson.

I decree highly positive word of mouth testimonials will drive sales and traffic to my business.

I decree my sales increase every week.

I decree December is always my highest-grossing month each year.

I decree I make sales 24 hours a day and am not limited in any way by standard business hours.

I decree everyone who visits my websites and business locations buys.

I decree I deliver quality and excellence above what's expected and as a result, my customers are loyal to my brand.

I decree I am, I can, and I will.

I decree I am wealthy, trailblazing CEO.

Today I release all and any sickness, I bless it for lessons, and I move on to health and abundance.

I decree I have all the energy I need to accomplish my goals.

Day by day, I am growing healthier and stronger.

I am living a long and healthy life.

I am active, energetic, and in control of my life.

As I grow in spiritual abundance, my health is renewed.

I am willing to learn how to build my business.

I am willing to work hard.

I am willing to serve fewer people to have a greater impact.

I am willing to operate with an abundance mindset.

I will persevere despite hard times.

Money comes to me easily every date I become more and more prosperous. Prosperity is RIGHT.

I am a magnet for money, I am prosperous and will always be prosperous because my Father in Heaven has already provided.

I am worthy of being paid for my gifts and talents. These gifts and talents were bestowed upon me to provide me the ability to care for me and my family.

I consistently attract people and act on opportunities that lead to more abundance.

I can manage large sums of money with grace.

Money creates freedom and the opportunities to help the world.

I have dominion over money, and I boldly accept all that the world has to offer me.

My finances are growing beyond my dreams, and I have the right tools and teams in place to direct this growth into the right avenues to provide for my children's children.

I am a good steward over all the abundance God has given me; I budget to spend wisely; I focus on ways to maximize my earnings and I sow sees into charities to make the world a better place because of me being in it.

May these decrees and declarations empower, motivate, and inspire you to unleash your brilliance, power, and resilience in the pursuit of business excellence.

Dr. Tschanna Taylor

Notes

Notes

Notes

Other Works by Dr. Tschanna Taylor

- *I S.E.E.-Lost Sight in One Eye but Didn't Lose Vision-Coming Summer '24*

- *From the Porch to Purpose: Recipes from Grandma to My Entrepreneurial Success-Coming Winter '24*

- *Brilliant, Powerful, & Resilient Business Planner-companion to Brilliant, Powerful & Resilient Book*

- *Brilliant, Powerful & Resilient: Unleashing Women's Business Excellence*

- *Go All In & Get the "F" Out*

- *Reaffirmed: Shed, Shift & Show Up: 15 Powerful Stories of Healing and Transformation*

- *Redefined: 21 Days to Reset Your Mind, Body & Soul Devotional*

- *Redefined: 21 Days to Reset Your Mind, Body & Soul Prayer Journal*

- *Redefined: 21 Days to Reset Your Mind, Body & Soul Notebook*

- *H.E.R. Extreme Makeover: Reflections of Healing, Equipping and Restoring Messes Into Masterpieces*

- *Promises for a Woman of Purpose Devotional & Coloring Pages*

- *Woman of Influence Prayer Journal*

- *After the Affair: Moving Forward God's Way*

Collaborations

- *Blooming Into Purpose; Out of the Ashes Into the Son-LaDeema Burns*

- *Turbulence: A Practical Guide On How To Remain Resilient In the Midst of Every Storm-Carla R. Cannon*

- *Affirmations that Strengthen Me-Dr. Marilyn Porter*

- *Being Woman-Schan Ellis*

- *Synergized Faith-Dr. Stevii Mills*

- *Borderline Fine: How to Find Time To Do It All For Women By Women-Gail Gardner*

- *The Professional Woman: Self-Esteem, Confidence, & Empowerment-Linda Eastman*

- *The Purposed Woman-360 Day Devotional-LaTasha Williams*

- *LeadHERship-13 Confident & Audacious Women Building Business God's Way-Sheya Chisenga*

- *I AM HEALED-Rhonda Watts Robinson*

- *Even As My Soul Prospers – Allison Arnett*

- *Prepare for Purpose- Sharvette Mitchell*

- *Building Wealth: Entrepreneurial, Professional, and Financial Expertise Unlocked-Ayanna Smith*

Brilliant, Powerful & Resilient: Unleashing Women's Business Excellence – A book collaboration to help women entrepreneurs dive deeper into strategies and stories of women who have transformed their businesses and lives.

Purchase your copy of the #1 Amazon Best-Seller, Brilliant, Powerful, & Resilient: Unleashing Women's Business Excellence here:

https://bit.ly/brilliantpowerfulresilientbook

ACKNOWLEDGMENTS

It would be impossible to thank everyone who has helped me take this book from passion to print but here are just a few...

My Savior: Thank you for chasing me down to focus on the assignment and to serve in the capacity in which you have entrusted me. Thank you for the honor of partnering with me to bring what I have learned to the world to create a movement and transform the world.

My Family and Friends: I couldn't do all what God has called me to do without your encouragement, support, and love. I'm forever grateful and love you all so much.

My Pastors & Spiritual Coverings: Thank you all for providing me with exemplary trainings so I can go out into the highways & hedges reaching the multitudes.

My publishing team: Thank you for working tirelessly to help see this project through to the end. To my publishing mentors for your wisdom and guidance as I continue to master my craft in the publishing industry.

And last, but certainly not least, thank you to YOU. Thank you for being a part of my community allowing me to serve you as you partner with God to change the world. Thank you for sharing glimpses of God's power as he directly answered/answers your prayers. Blessings to all you endeavor for the Kingdom!

ABOUT THE AUTHOR

Dr. Tschanna Taylor

Dr. Tschanna Taylor®, also known as "The Publishing & Marketing Powerhouse," is indeed a woman after God's own heart. As an entrepreneur for over 30 years in business, human resource management, and accounting, she's committed to helping others redefine their life and confidently share their stories to increase their impact, influence, and income.

With her transparent, yet strategic approach, Dr. Tschanna is committed to empowering global men and women with the tools to equip them to use their unique voices, stories, and expertise to redefine the marketplace.

Tschanna is a certified life and business strategist, marketplace chaplain, 13x international best-selling author, and speaker. Tschanna holds several degrees and certifications from DeVry University, Keller Graduate School of Management, Liberty University, and other institutions, focusing on counseling, coaching, and entrepreneurship.

Dr. Tschanna currently runs and operates Tschanna Taylor® Enterprises, LLC, which houses Emerald Tree Press, Redefined Woman International Network, and Wealthy Trailblazing CEO's. Set apart by her transparent delivery and transformative storytelling abilities, anyone can see that she is resilient about helping others operate authentically and unapologetically in their God-given purpose.

Learn more @tschannataylor on Facebook, Instagram, and Tik Tok. Visit her website at www.tschannataylor.com or https://www.tschanna.com/.

Direct email inquiries: info@tschannataylor.com